Primitive Ego Psychology
For
Life Coaches & Mental Health Counselors

Taming the Primitive Ego

THE MANIFESTO OF A THERAPIST/LIFE COACH

The Journey toward Middlepath Thinking
and Growth in Self-Awareness

by Dick Rauscher

A Stonyhill Publication

Copyright © 2016 Dick Rauscher
All rights reserved.
ISBN:1539678032
ISBN-13:9781539678038

CONTENTS

PREFACE 1

INTRODUCTION 5

MY JOURNEY 9

    THE THREE INSIGHTS THAT MOST SHAPED THE BIRTH OF PRIMITIVE EGO PSYCHOLOGY 11

THE BIRTH OF CHILDHOOD PRIMITIVE EGO DUALISTIC THINKING 19

    OUR CHILDHOOD PRIMITIVE EGO IS THE UNCONSCIOUS OPERATING SYSTEM OF OUR MIND 20

    THREE REALITY DISTORTING BELIEFS OF A PRIMITIVE EGO 22

BEGINNING THE JOURNEY TOWARD THE "WHOLENESS" OF REALITY AND NON-DUAL THINKING 27

    SCIENCE: NON-DUALITY IN THE OBJECTIVE REALM 27

    BELIEFS: NON-DUALITY IN THE SUBJECTIVE 29

WHY THESE CONCEPTS ARE IMPORTANT FOR LIFE COACHES AND MENTAL HEALTH COUNSELORS 35

    WHERE TO BEGIN AS A LIFE COACH 39

    BECOMING AN EFFECTIVE LIFE COACH 40

PRACTICES FOR THE JOURNEY TOWARD SELF-AWARENESS AND TAMING YOUR CHILDHOOD PRIMITIVE EGO 43

    STAGES OF AWAKENING 46

WHY I WROTE THIS MANIFESTO 49

ADDENDUM: WHY I BELIEVE PRIMITIVE EGO PSYCHOLOGY IS SO IMPORTANT 51

PREFACE

Changing A Client's Worldview Is A Process

I wrote this Manifesto to support the on-going continuing education of Professional Life Coaches, Life Coaching students, and Mental Health Counselors. Learning how to help our client is a process that requires developing the skills and insights needed to help our clients tame their childhood primitive ego. Changing the *way* our clients think requires knowing *what* they think (their childhood primitive ego's self-limiting beliefs) and *how* they think (their childhood primitive ego's assumptions and illusions about reality).

Continuing education is a never-ending process given the rapidly changing knowledge of human psychology and behavior.

A successful life coaching or mental health counseling practice requires a lifetime commitment to continuing education and advanced professional training so we can better understand what gets in the way of our clients achieving their goals and dreams…..the unconscious obstacles that keep the client from living the life they want to live.

This Manifesto is an introduction to **Primitive Ego Psychology** and the *taming of our childhood primitive ego*. When our clients get stuck on the journey toward their goals, the problem is almost always *an unconscious childhood primitive ego belief distorting the way they think.* The evolution of Primitive Ego Psychology has been the primary focus of my thirty-year professional career; thirty years of training, education, and experience working with clients as a life coach, writer, and mental health counselor.

To become a successful life coach or mental health counselor for our clients, it is essential that we understand ourselves through *growth in self-awareness.* The more I have been able to identify and incorporate primitive ego theory into my professional and personal life, the more effective I have been in helping others. I am grateful every day for the ways primitive ego theory has helped shape who I am… and how it has helped my clients overcome the mental obstacles that threatened to overwhelm their goals and dreams. Taming the childhood primitive ego and *growth in self-awareness are essential* for *anyone* whose goal in life is…

- embracing happiness,
- creating a successful life,
- developing happy relationships,
- achieving their life goals, and
- creating the life they've dreamed of living.

Helping our client's *tame their primitive ego* and achieve their life goals requires that life coaches and mental health counselors…

a) learn to embrace the *wisdom and meaning in life* that comes from our own journey into *deeper self-awareness*;
b) gain a deeper understanding *how our mind works*, and
c) learn the specific skills and insights required to *tame our own childhood primitive ego.*

Awakening our consciousness and achieving growth in self-awareness are best achieved when we know how our mind works; including how we think and what we think. Why?

Because, just like our clients, *we too use our minds to create our lives and our world.*

So it makes sense the more we know about the childhood conditioning of *our* mind and how *we* think, the more choice we will have in how we use it! And most importantly, *we can't teach our clients what we don't know ourselves… what we haven't experienced.*

Knowing how the human mind thinks is essential if we want to be a successful life coach or mental health counselor and help our clients achieve their goals.

This is also true for our clients! *They can't change what they don't understand and accept about themselves.*

Awakening our consciousness and achieving growth in self-awareness are best achieved when we know how our mind works; including how we think and what we think.

Learning to embrace reality and awaken our human consciousness are one-in-the-same subject. They both require *knowing* how our mind works and *what our minds believe to be true*. This knowledge happens only when we have *intentionally* embraced growth in self-awareness and learned to *tame our own childhood primitive ego*.

Awakening the human consciousness, and the growth in self-awareness required to tame our childhood primitive ego, happen when we have *the courage to take action*... when we learn to *change how we think*... when we learn to:

- become self-aware of our reality distorting *childhood beliefs and conditioning,*
- empty our primitive ego of its *need to be "right,"*
- drop our primitive ego's *dualistic "us vs. them" thinking,*
- embrace a more evolved *non-dual, both/and consciousness,*
- transform our conscious and dropped the dangerous *illusion of separateness,*
- embrace "we" thinking and the concepts of *"mutual benefit"* and *"common good"* for all living beings.

When The Client Gets Stuck

When our clients get stuck on the journey toward their goals, we need to help them better understand *why* they're stuck, and *what they need to do* to get unstuck. For over thirty years, primitive ego theory has reminded me almost daily that *we can't teach others what we haven't learned ourselves*. We can't lead others into the wilderness of their unconscious primitive ego *until we have made the journey ourselves*.

A successful life coach requires deep insight on *how* the client thinks when the client is stuck on the journey toward their goals. Successful life coaches and mental health counselors know how to support the client's journey into a deeper self-awareness... *because they had the courage to make that journey themselves.*

Welcome to Primitive Ego Psychology

This Manifesto was written to introduce you to Primitive Ego Psychology and help you deepen the *professional skills* and *personal self-awareness* required to become a successful life coach or mental health counselor. Like our clients, *we too struggle to awaken to the presence of our own unconscious primitive ego.* Our ability to help others improves dramatically when we have learned to tame our own primitive ego.

My purpose in writing this Manifesto is to support and encourage your growth in self-awareness as a life coach or mental health counselor. Your clients will thank you for your willingness to have already grown in the same way you are helping them to grow.

Dick Rauscher, Redmond, Oregon 2016

INTRODUCTION

Most people struggle.........
- to experience a lasting sense of happiness,
- to create healthy relationships,
- to achieve greater purpose in life, and
- to live lives of deeper meaning,

but they fail to grasp the reality that we can not achieve our life goals *by searching for them in the outer world.*

Life coaches and mental health counselors know those frantically sought goals of the client will only be realized when the client has embraced the courage to *look inward* and become more *self-aware*; when the client has learned to tame their primitive ego and the unconscious, "self-limiting" reality distorting beliefs they learned in childhood. Life coaches and mental health counselors know the answers and insights the client is searching for can only be found when they have embraced the courage to journey into the wilderness of their inner world and listen to the quiet whispers of their soul.

Life coaches and mental health counselors understand the reality that *every experience* we have in our lives is the *experience of a relationship in one form or another*. And they also know *that the most important relationship we will ever experience is the relationship we have with ourselves.*

Deepening the skills and insights needed to add value to the lives of others requires life coaches and mental health counselors to better understand and deepen their self-awareness; the ability to *see, accept, and then tame their own childhood primitive ego.* They understand that *you can't teach what you don't know.* You can't lead others into the wilderness until you've discovered the courage to take the *inward journey* and deepened your own *self-awareness;* until you've *tamed your own* childhood primitive ego.

...every experience we have in our lives is the experience of a relationship in one form or another........ the most important relationship we will ever experience is the relationship we have with ourselves.

If this makes sense to you, if your goal is a desire to improve your life coaching skills and your mental health counseling skills so you can be more effective in adding value to the lives of others… this Manifesto was written for you.

This Manifesto is meant to shift the way you look at reality… and yourself.

We all carry reality distorting beliefs from childhood into our adult life. We all do it. It's part of being human. Being an effective and successful life coach requires taming our childhood primitive ego. It requires diving deeply into our own *self-*awareness… learning to pay attention to *how,* and *what we* think. How we look at life and reality. *Until we have learned to shift our attention on how and what we think, our ability to understand and help our clients achieve their goals will be seriously limited.* We will quickly become frustrated at our inability to successfully "hold" a client while they learn about themselves and the skills they need to reach their goal. Client turnover will be high. Success as a life coach will be low.

Successful life coaching is not a "technique" one uses. It is knowing how your client thinks. But that insight can't be intellection *learned*; it has to be *experienced personally* by our own journey into the subtleties and reality distorting beliefs of our own childhood primitive ego.

This Manifesto is an invitation to begin that journey inward. It will take you take you step by step through some of the basic insights and teachings of Primitive Ego Psychology and primitive ego theory. It's meant to be an introduction to primitive ego theory, not an in-depth training course. It will give you some of the skills and information you will need to help your clients tame *their* primitive ego through *their* growth in self-awareness, by helping you improve *your* ability to deepen *your* self-awareness.

Self-Awareness is learning to pay attention to how, and what we think. Until we have learned to shift our attention on how and what we think, our ability to understand and help our clients achieve their goals will be seriously limited.

Important Concepts

- Evolving our consciousness and becoming more self-aware is *hard work*. It requires courage because much of what we learn about ourselves will challenge our self-identity. We rarely like what we discover about ourselves when we become more self-aware. That's why we keep it hidden in our unconscious. Self-awareness is not a one-time learning. It requires learning about ourselves over and over......until we finally get it and accept what we've discovered. You'll know when that happens; it's called humility.
- Our ego *does not like change*. It resists change even when we want to grow and evolve. Growth in self-awareness and awakening our human consciousness to the presence of our childhood primitive ego is a process that takes time. Learning to become an effective life coach is also a process. They both take time and effort.
- This Manifesto will offer the reader a map of some of the changes necessary to become a more successful self-aware life coach or mental health counselor... *but the map is never the*

journey itself. Reading a menu is not the same as eating the meal. Until we have the courage to *take our own journey* into deeper self-awareness, we will never develop the skills and insights that only come from the experience of actually taking the journey inward.

- Our primitive ego is filled with *reality distorting views, illusions, and beliefs from childhood*. At the end of this Manifesto, I have included a list of some additional childhood skills and insights that I believe are important for us to wrestle with on our journey into self-awareness. The further you journey into the wilderness of your own childhood primitive ego, the more helpful you will be to your clients… and the more successful you'll be as a life coach or mental health counselor.

MY JOURNEY

A 12th century Nasrudin story:

Nasrudin was frantically riding his donkey up and down the streets of his small village one morning. After watching Nasrudin for a while, one of the villagers yelled out "Nasrudin, Nasrudin, what are you doing so frantically riding your donkey up and down the village streets?"

Nasrudin looked back over his shoulder and shouted back "What am I doing? What am I doing? You fool... I'm looking for my donkey!"

The problem that keeps us from the happiness and meaning we long for, the problem that keeps us from taming our primitive ego and creating a more awakened human consciousness, is much like Nasrudin's donkey. Our childhood primitive ego is so close to us... so much a part of us... we fail to see it.

How My Journey As A Life Coach/Therapist Began

I began my adult life as a dualistic, black and white, either/or thinker; it was me against the world. And of course, because my inner-child was convinced all good things come from the world, I *knew* happiness would come to me if I were famous, wealthy, and successful in my Electrical Engineering career. My goal was to be a millionaire by the time I was thirty. I was well on my way to achieving those career goals by the time I was thirty-two ... but I awoke one day to the sobering reality that I wasn't happy. I wasn't living the life I wanted to live. So I quit the corporate life.

So much for the dream of a successful career and wealth.

Fast Forward A Few Years ...

I woke up the morning of my 35th birthday, threw some wood in the wood stove, and headed to the barn to milk the goats, feed the chickens, and slop the pigs. I was homesteading on 27 acres in upstate New York raising a family of six on $7000 a year.

Fast Forward a Few More Years ...

It was a warm summer evening in the late 1970's when the universe introduced me to the *"rest of my life."* An innocent philosophic question was about to change my world. My days of milking goats, building stone walls, rough sawn wood barns, and racing a dirt bike in cross-country "endurance" races were about to become a fond memory.

Like most Saturday evenings in the summer, we were sitting around a campfire drinking beer and making music with five or six neighboring families. The kids were playing kick the can in the field down near the pond.

The musical instruments were back in their cases, and we had settled into quiet conversations about life and philosophy. *Talking about philosophy after a few beers around a campfire is a lot like getting into a taxi and impulsively telling the driver "just drive"... you have absolutely no idea where you're going to end up.*

The guitar player picked up his beer, looked slowly around the campfire, and asked an innocent philosophic question. "So what would you do with your life if you could do anything you wanted to do with it."

When it came to my turn to answer the question, I impulsively responded: "I would be a Pastor." Talk about a show stopper. The only sound for the next thirty seconds was the crackling of the burning campfire. To this day, I have no idea where those words came from, but over the next few months, I couldn't get them out of my head.

The following spring I signed up for some courses at Colgate-Rochester Seminary to explore the possibility that I might actually enter the Christian ministry. I tried hard to fit in theologically, but my degree in Electrical Engineering and Physics made it hard for me to accept much of what I was being taught.

It wasn't long before the more conservative students made it a point to avoid me in the cafeteria. Their fear, I think, was the possibility that my questions and theological doubts might be contagious.

I began to have serious doubts about my decision to enter the ministry.

The seminary felt like home to me. I loved learning and the sense of community, but my struggle with Christian theology was growing. The traditional conservative Christian beliefs that embraced scientifically illiterate, first-century worldviews lacked the spiritual wisdom and insights I hungered for. At the same time, the desire to grow spiritually was an inner calling I couldn't ignore.

I didn't want to live a life that simply happened to me. I didn't want to live a life that others had chosen for me. I wanted to discover the truth for myself. I wanted to discover for myself why I was here, what my soul had come here to do? What it was that I was meant to contribute to the world? I knew I wanted to add value to the world; not just take up space.

These were the inner conflicts, doubts, thoughts, and questions that I was wrestling with the morning I walked into my first class in Pastoral Counseling 101... and *knew* that I had finally discovered the path I was born to walk.

And, as they say, the rest is history.

I left corporate life and went "back to the land" in search of happiness and meaning; to figure out who I was. Homesteading the land for those five years was *"the"* rebirthing experience my soul had been searching for. It was the first step of an amazing journey that eventually took me toward a seminary M.Div. Degree; ordination as an Elder in the United Methodist Church; working as a Chaplain and Counselor at Keuka College in upstate New York; an AAPC Fellowship in analytic psychotherapy; and eventually over two decades working in private practice as a mental health therapist and life coach helping people find meaning in their lives, encouraging them to discover their life purpose, and walking with them as they struggled to discover and embrace the authentic life that called them.

THE THREE INSIGHTS THAT MOST SHAPED THE BIRTH OF PRIMITIVE EGO PSYCHOLOGY

I had a successful therapy practice underway, but I saw that the technical, psycho-therapeutic language I had been taught, was not helping my clients move toward the healing and growth they longed for in their lives. It was too technical. Too removed from my client's experience of life to be helpful. I needed a therapeutic language that *made sense* to my client's.

Insight #1: Survival Skills

When I learned about the concept of *"childhood survival skills,"* I realized my clients were not dealing with neurotic behaviors and character disorders. They were essentially attempting to use the survival skills learned in early childhood to navigate their adult lives.

For the first time, I could "see" the two primary *survival skills* creating conflict and unhappiness in my client's lives;

- *dualistic, black and white, either/or, good and bad thinking of childhood, and*
- *their primitive ego's need to be "right."*

I recognized that dualistic childhood primitive ego thinking and the need to be right were not only creating conflict and unhappiness in the lives of my clients, they were also responsible for the conflict and pain I experienced in my own life as well. They were the two childhood primitive ego beliefs responsible for most of the conflict and pain we experience in life and especially in our relationships with others.

Insight #2: Humility

The second insight that changed the way I see the world began the day I decided to retire from homesteading and return to the modern world. What I learned in the years following that decision was how hard it is to climb out of poverty and re-enter modern society ... even when that poverty has been self-imposed.

I had a bachelor's degree in Electrical Engineering. I was living on 27 acres in upstate New York fifty-five miles from the nearest large city. My home was a small 12' x 20' foot cabin five hundred feet above the valley floor. A hand pump on the front porch supplied the "running water." We had a two-hole outhouse with a great view of the valley, and an indoor compost toilet. What I *didn't* have was a financial base to support a wife and four children without the income that had been provided by the farm.

PRIMITIVE EGO PSYCHOLOGY

We had been living on less than seven thousand dollars a year for half a decade. This was a level of income that was adequate while we were self-sufficient and living off of the land, but woefully inadequate without the food and financial income provided by our homesteading efforts.

The struggle to get back on my feet taught me humility and created in me a deep compassion for the poor in our world. I was well educated and owned property, but I had no cash to get traction. Without cash, making the transition from self-sufficient homesteading to purchasing food in a grocery store became a financial nightmare. To this day, I emotionally hesitate to answer the phone in fear that it will be another creditor demanding payment or threatening legal action.

When I hear people tell the poor, just get a job, and life will be fine, I know that's not true. Digging out of poverty was an almost overwhelming challenge.

When you are starting from poverty, getting traction to make the journey toward prosperity and success is all but impossible. I shudder to think what it must feel like to begin that journey as a disadvantaged person with limited resources. It was a five-year struggle for me, and I had resources most of the poor, and disadvantaged can only dream about. Learning to accept the grace and compassion of friends who were willing to reach out and offer me a helping hand when the journey overwhelmed me was a major challenge. Without their help during those days as I struggled to get back on my feet, I'm not sure where I would be today. And I had a college engineering degree!

The humility born in that life experience changed forever the way I see the world and the plight of the poor. The struggle to eliminate "*us vs. them*" thinking created by the illusion of separateness in the world is a very personal issue for me.

Eliminating dualistic "*us vs. them*" thinking, the illusion of separateness, and increasing our human ability to offer compassion to those less fortunate, is a primary reason why I became a writer and life coach/mental health counselor. The "why" of my life purpose for the last thirty years has been a focus on adding value to the lives of others, awakening the human consciousness to the presence of our childhood primitive ego, and teaching others the skills and insights needed to successfully tame the childhood primitive ego. In other words, becoming more self-aware, and helping others do the same. Without deep *self-*awareness, and the ability to tame our childhood primitive ego that comes from the journey into *self-*awareness, happiness and success in life are all but impossible to achieve.

Insight #3: Non-Duality

The third insight that changed my life was *non-duality* and *non-dual thinking.*

I had the head wisdom from the first two insights. I even had the beginning of the deeper heart wisdom I needed to better care for and support the emotional and spiritual growth of my clients. But coming from an engineering background, I still saw the world in fragmented, bits and pieces of reality. I was not yet *"seeing"* the *wholeness* of reality and creation.

Like Nasrudin's donkey, and my own childhood primitive ego, that simple reality called "wholeness" was so close I couldn't *see* it.

Awakening to the non-dual wholeness of reality happened when my study of Buddhist psychology changed my spiritual worldview from theological, religious beliefs, and technical human developmental theory, to the deeper wisdom that our *"true-self"* is not our *"ego-self."*

- We are not a unique "self" separate from the rest of the universe as our unconscious childhood primitive ego would have us believe.
- We are not the unconscious primitive ego "self" born in the childhood crucible of black and white, right and wrong dualistic thinking.
- We are not just our body, and a mind filled with thoughts, emotions, beliefs, opinions, assumptions, expectations and hurts.
- We are not a "self" defined by our possessions and the various experiences we have had as a "separate" and unique being. That separate ego-"self" is an illusion called our false-self.
- Our "true self"… who we "are"… is a pure observing consciousness.

It was finally clear to me. Our inner child's dualistic primitive ego, an ego that turns the rest of creation into categories of "them" or "other," lacks the insight and non-dual maturity needed to embrace the unity, oneness, and wholeness of reality.

The dualistic thinking of our childhood primitive ego; the dualistic thinking process created by the illusion of separateness, is and always has been, one of humanity's greatest dangers and threat. It creates unhappiness, destroys relationships, is the source of judgmental prejudice, and is responsible for most of the conflict and violence we experience in the world both currently and historically.

For the first time, I could see how dualistic "us vs. them" thinking, and the violence it creates, stops our ability to evolve an authentic, compassionate, awakened human consciousness dead in its tracks. It blinds our consciousness; our ability to see, embrace and accept the unity and oneness of reality.

If we don't learn to awaken our human consciousness to;

a. the presence of our dualistic primitive ego,
b. the illusion of separateness,
c. learn to become more self-aware, and
d. begin to embrace a true non-dual consciousness…

the *ability to achieve an awakened human* consciousness will not be difficult… *it will be impossible.*

The dualistic thinking of our childhood primitive ego; the dualistic thinking process created by the illusion of separateness, is and always has been, one of humanity's greatest dangers and threat.

Stated simply, the belief that we are a separate "self" or "i" is a powerful and dangerous illusion of our childhood primitive ego; an illusion that will continue to create most of the suffering we experience in life until we have;

a. grown in self-awareness;

b. awakened to the *reality distorting beliefs* of our childhood primitive ego consciousness,
c. learned to embrace the *wholeness of reality*, and
d. intentionally emptied our childhood primitive ego consciousness of the reality distorting illusion that our *"self"* is *an object separate from the rest of reality.*

It is the *illusion of separateness* that so often drives our obsessive human need to *embrace greed* and our never-ending focus on *what's in it for "me"*. It is the illusion of separateness that drives a wedge into all of our relationships; a wedge that separates our "self" from the rest of the universe.

The primitive ego's illusion of separateness is also directly responsible for the greed that drives our "us vs. them" global economic system.

The only antidote to *greed* is a consciousness that has learned to drop the illusion of separateness and learned how to embrace a *"we"/"us" focus*... a focus on the *common good*, and *mutual benefit* for the "*whole*."

Only a true, non-dual, awakened consciousness that embraces deep self-awareness, the wholeness of creation... an awakened, non-dual consciousness that refuses to fragment reality into judgmental categories of "us" vs. "them"... has the power to create a non-violent, compassionate, awakened world.

Where I Am Today

With this third insight, I finally *knew* the life purpose I was meant to embrace was exploring, teaching, and writing about;

- the humility, self-awareness, and emptiness of ego required to achieve an authentic, *awakened human conscious…* and create true happiness in life.
- the *self-awareness* required for us to empty our childhood primitive ego and let go of the dualistic "false self" of childhood that thinks it knows how the universe *"should"* function. In other words, awakening our consciousness to the presence of our inner child's primitive ego and its tendency to *"push the river"* by assuming we know what *"should be"* and ignoring the reality of *"what is."*
- the intentional evolution of a true non-dual human consciousness that embraces "mutual benefit" through its *interconnection and interdependence* with the rest of creation. A consciousness that has learned to live in *right relationship with the laws of nature* and the natural world.

The journey to become a *non-dual thinker* has been the most exciting, meaningful but difficult journey I have ever undertaken.

The further I've journeyed toward an awakened consciousness and *non-duality*, the more I am discovering the lack of stress that comes when I have the courage to embrace change more openly. When I intentionally become more self-aware and let go of *the idea that my subjective ego beliefs represent absolute truth.*

I have more to learn on this journey toward an awakened consciousness. Fortunately, there are those in our community who have been on this path far longer than myself. Those enlightened souls willing to share their spiritual wisdom include folks like Bernadette Robert's, Alan Watts, Wendell Berry, Beatrice Bruteau, Andrew Cohen, Steve McIntosh, Anthony DeMello, Eckhart Tolle, the Dali Lama, Tich Nhat Hahn, Peter Russell, and of course, all of humanity's great spiritual teachers, mystics, and sages.

They are humanity's awakened trailblazers and guides teaching us about *"emptiness of ego"* and guiding us through the *wilderness of our childhood primitive ego psyches* as we journey toward *self-awareness* and our *true-self*. They are the teachers that support and encourage us when we encounter the inevitable challenges that are part of the journey toward our *full humanity*.

I am increasingly thankful for the heart wisdom they offer.

THE BIRTH OF CHILDHOOD PRIMITIVE EGO DUALISTIC THINKING

The black and white, dualistic, either/or thinking, we all learned in childhood, is an early developmental stage of childhood. As young children, we sensed that everything ... whether good or bad ... seemed to come to us from the world. We *knew* we were powerless, so pleasing our caretakers was seen as critical.

To accomplish that task, we split the world into the simple dualistic categories of good and bad, right and wrong, pleasure and pain. We learned very quickly that good and right brought more pleasure than bad and wrong. If we were "good" or "right" we were rewarded. If we were "bad," or "wrong" we were punished. We were learning to survive childhood.

At about seven years of age, our basic self-identity was complete. *We were able to experience ourselves as a unique "self" ... a "self" or "i" separate from everyone else.* Our *"me"* was born.

Developmentally, the *primitive ego* of our *inner-child* and everything we'd learned about life began to slide quietly, like cozy slippers on a thick carpet, into our unconscious... *including our illusion of separateness.*

I will never forget the day I picked up my son from school. He got in the car and excitedly told me that he realized that he was the *only* "him" in the whole world. Outwardly, I shared the excitement of his amazing insight. Inwardly, I experienced sadness knowing that his self-identity was beginning its slide into his unconscious. All I could think about was whether I had done a good job in helping him create a healthy sense of "self"... a "self" that was interconnected and interdependent on the rest of creation.

OUR CHILDHOOD PRIMITIVE EGO IS THE UNCONSCIOUS OPERATING SYSTEM OF OUR MIND

A simple way to think about the primitive ego of our inner-child is using the analogy of an operating system in our computer. The operating system of our computer is pretty much invisible, but without that operating system, our computer would not function. Everything we do or create on our computer is controlled by that invisible operating system. *Until the day, we awaken to its presence, the primitive ego of our inner-child will be the unconscious operating system controlling who we are, and how we function in the world.*

Until we become intentionally self-aware and awaken our mind to a higher, more evolved adult level of consciousness... *the unconscious primitive ego of our inner-child will continue to use* its childhood beliefs and learning's to unconsciously *split* the world into the dualistic categories of;

- *"me"* vs. the rest of the world,
- right from wrong, and
- good from bad.

We will look like adults. We will behave like adults most of the time. However, emotionally, we will be seven-year-old children pretending to look and act like adults. We know it is important to be compassionate, so we try to be compassionate. We try to show the world what we think the world wants to see. However, our façade of compassion will quickly disappear the moment our primitive ego feels its self-identity, beliefs, and opinions are being challenged or threatened.

Until we become self-aware, we will look like adults, but behave as 7-year-old children fighting on the playground.

PRIMITIVE EGO PSYCHOLOGY

When we feel threatened, our primitive ego will immediately begin to unconsciously "knee-jerk" a negative, defensive, survival-of-the-fittest energy into the world. *Our childhood primitive ego will emotionally insist that we are "right" and the other person is wrong.* The result? Our dualistic right and wrong thinking will begin to clash with the dualistic right and wrong thinking of the *other person* and quickly escalate into conflict and emotional violence ... or worse.

A Personal Example

When we moved into our new home some years ago, one of our new neighbors came over with a welcoming dinner. She was always the first to wave and offer a cheerful hello in the morning. Then one day before the national elections she began talking about her favorite candidate and some of the controversial issues in that election. When I failed to agree with some of her views, she turned around, went into her house, closed the door, and we have not had a conversation since that time.

The primitive ego of our inner-child is the unconscious operating system that controls who we are, and how we function in the world.

It's a rare person who doesn't have to tiptoe carefully around a "brittle" relative or acquaintance   e who claims to be "*compassionate.*" But we *know* it's best to avoid discussions about politics, religion, global warming, abortion, immigration, immunization, or affordable care when they are around.

Families frequently have stories of conflict and pain caused by dualistic thinking. For example, Carl grew up in a family that believed in the traditional family values. The father of three children, he frequently voiced his strong anti-gay opinions and bias. When his only daughter announced that she was gay, Carl had to choose between his inflexible black-and-white beliefs... or risk the reality of losing his relationship with her. This is a painful story that plays out all too often in our black and white homophobic culture.

Black and white dualistic thinking will continue creating conflict in our life and our relationships with others until we;

- have the courage to *direct our attention inward and begin the inner spiritual journey required to increase our self-awareness.*
- recognize the presence of our own primitive ego and its *illusion of separateness* and *need to be "right."*
- intentionally awaken our consciousness to the *reality distorting beliefs* and "beams" in our own eye.
- Recognize that we are *interdependent and interconnected* with all of creation.
- Embrace a *focus on the whole* "we," and the concept of *"mutual benefit."*

THREE REALITY DISTORTING BELIEFS OF A PRIMITIVE EGO

1) Dualistic thinking:

- Our childhood primitive ego insists on *fragmenting the world* into categories of "this vs.that," hot vs. cold, up vs. down, good vs. bad, in vs. out. *The fragmentation of the world into bits and pieces is a never-ending process for our primitive ego.*
- Dualistic thinking is a *primary source of unhappiness and conflict* in our lives, and it's only found inside the human mind.
- Dualistic thinking is the unconscious need of our inner child's primitive ego to split the world into the *dualistic* categories of *good* and *bad*; *right* and *wrong*,
- Dualism and dualistic splitting, *"you* vs. *me"* and *"us vs. them"* thinking, is the taproot feeding the tree of *extremism* in our world today….and the fruit of *extremism* is always conflict and violence because our childhood primitive ego always needs to be "right." (See #3 below.)
- The conflict, violence, and lack of civility created by *ideological extremism* resulting from *dualistic primitive ego thinking* are

clearly doing violence to the souls of the world... both individually and collectively.
- Solving the problems created by the *ideological extremism* of dualistic thinking will be impossible until we understand that the root source of the violence in the world is our childhood primitive ego's subjective *"us vs. them"* thinking... *born in the illusion of separateness.*

2) The Illusion of Separateness:
- The dualistic categories of *"you* vs. *me"* or *"us vs. them"* are created by our childhood primitive ego's dangerous subjective belief in the *illusion of individual separateness*.....in contrast with an evolved, awakened adult consciousness *that embraces the "wholeness of reality."*
- The childhood primitive ego believes that our *"self" is separate from the rest of the universe.* This illusion of separateness; the sense that we are a unique and separate *"me"* was created by our unconscious childhood primitive ego at about seven years of age.
- The illusion of separateness creates greed and "what's in it for *me*" thinking.

3) The Never-Ending Need To Be Right:
- Our childhood primitive ego assumes we are always "good" and "right." It has a never-ending need to *always* be *"right!"*
- Our childhood primitive ego does not have the ability *to embrace the changes* needed for us to create a more evolved, enlightened, and awakened human consciousness. *Change* implies to our childhood primitive ego that it was somehow *"wrong."*
- Change threatens the *"rightness"* of our beliefs. Our self-identity, *who we are*, is based on our beliefs and our worldviews. Change threatens to deconstruct our childhood primitive ego's sense of "self" or self-identity.

There are many more reality distorting beliefs that are held as absolute truth by the childhood primitive ego. We'll look at a few more of them in the Chapters below. The important things to remember at this

point are;
- the concept that *any belief, conscious or unconscious, that distorts reality in any way* will *always* create pain, suffering, unhappiness, stress, anxiety, conflict, and violence for both for the holder of the belief, and often for others. It's called pushing the river. Reality, of course, is the river.
- The problem is not just *what* our client's thinks, it's also *how* they think. Childhood primitive ego beliefs that distort reality are almost always unconscious attempts to push the river. Pushing the river or attempting to force reality to conform to our subjective beliefs and assumptions *about* reality… *never* works out well. *When a client is stuck and failing to achieve the goals they want in their lives, it's a good bet that there is an unconscious, reality distorting childhood belief at work inside their thinking.* A primary task of the life coach and mental health counseling is helping the client uncover those reality distorting childhood primitive ego beliefs so they can continue to grow and move toward their goals.
- Learn to pay attention when the client uses the words "Yea, but". They almost always point to a power struggle between the client's goals and their unconscious reality distorting beliefs from childhood. Until the client recognizes that the problem is internal, it often becomes a power struggle that the client projects onto the life coach or mental health counselor who is attempting to help them achieve their stated goals.
- *Knowing* something does not mean that we have the skills to actually *live into* and manifest that knowledge in the world. Everything discussed in this Manifesto is about you the life coach/mental health counselor, *and* your client. I will not differentiate as to who I am talking about in the material that follows. Remember the adage *"you can't teach what you don't know. You can't lead another any further into the wilderness than you have journeyed yourself. If you try, it will only be the blind leading the blind."*

PRIMITIVE EGO PSYCHOLOGY

This Manifesto is meant to be a map of the inward journey that we *all* have to take if our goal is success and happiness. In other words, we *all* have to take the inward journey... *especially if we are called to a life coaching or mental health counseling profession that attempts to awaken the client's consciousness and add value to their lives.*

When a client is stuck and failing to achieve the goals they want in their lives, it's a good bet that there is an unconscious, reality distorting childhood belief at work inside their thinking.

BEGINNING THE JOURNEY TOWARD THE "WHOLENESS" OF REALITY AND NON-DUAL THINKING

> **Non-duality is**
> learning to see the unity and wholeness of reality and creation rather than the fragmented bits and pieces of reality called this vs. that, good vs. bad, or right vs. wrong… the either/or dualism in human thinking embedded in the childhood primitive ego.

Let me briefly explain what I mean by non-duality and non-dual thinking.

SCIENCE: NON-DUALITY IN THE OBJECTIVE REALM

It is easy to understand non-duality when we talk about the oneness or wholeness of our universe or creation. Science is teaching us that objective reality *"is"* non-dual. In our universe, *there is only one, not two.*

Everything in our evolving universe (from the largest galaxies to the smallest, quantum, subatomic particles) are an interconnected and interdependent part of the oneness or unity we refer to as creation.

We use human words to describe the *objective* polarities that occur in nature and our universe.

For example:

Hot vs. Cold	both words describe aspects of the same non-dual reality called temperature
In vs. Out Up vs. Down	both words describe aspects of the same non-dual reality called relative relationship or position
Light vs. Dark	both words describe aspects of the same non-dual reality called light/absence of light.
Matter vs. Space	both words describe fundamental aspects of the same energy that exist in our universe.

We can eliminate the word on one end of an "objective scientific polarity," but it *will* make the word on the other end of the polarity meaningless. We can change the words used to describe an objective scientific polarity, but it will not change the *non-dual unity or oneness* that the words are attempting to describe. For example;

- If we destroy *cold*, we destroy the meaning of *hot*, but *"temperature"* is not changed.
- If we destroy the concept of *in*, the concept of *out* ceases to have meaning, but the *"relative relationship"* is not changed.

As I stated previously, in our universe there is only one, not two. Nothing exists or acts on its own. Without others, there is no "self." Non-duality always honors the opposition.

Every "thing" in our universe is a non-dual, inter-connected, interdependent part of the same unity and wholeness called creation.

Science studies the bits and pieces of reality *to understand the physical laws* that make up our universe. However, our scientists understand, and fully embrace, the non-dual, interconnected, and interdependent wholeness and oneness of the specific reality they are studying. They *"see"* the universe, and the specific subject they are studying, through the eyes of a *non-dual consciousness*.

They understand that differentiation is not separation.

BELIEFS: NON-DUALITY IN THE SUBJECTIVE

"Subjective," means the beliefs, views, thoughts, and opinions of a person *are based on personal experiences, feelings, tastes, or assumptions.* In other words, the person's beliefs, views, and opinions are highly subjective or stated differently.....they are *"dependent on that individual's personal experience or perception for their existence."* *Every experience we have in life is a subjective relationship with a particular aspect of reality.*

For example, a temperature of 70 degrees is an objective reality, but *subjectively* it may feel warm to one person and cold to another.

Every experience we have in life is a subjective relationship with a particular aspect of reality.

Dualistic thinking is a powerful ability when it comes to science and increasing our understanding of the universe and the various laws that make our universe function: in other words when we are talking about the *non-duality* of objective, real things. However, when we talk about *non-duality* in the *subjective* realm of human beliefs, opinions, and assumptions that *reflect our human values... non-duality means something very different.* In the subjective realm, our ability to *"think"* about our *"thinking"* can create some serious problems when combined with dualistic thinking.

Truths Vs. Faith

For example, subjective "faith" and objective "truth" are two very different things. A person's subjective views, beliefs, and opinions may reflect their *faith* that they are *true*, but they are still *"subjective,"* and, therefore, *cannot be presented in the imperative voice of absolute truth.*

In science, *truth is "not" subjective...* it is always *objective, scientifically verifiable, measurable,* and *repeatable.* In science, *"truth"* is always open to, and even *invites,* the possibility of revision as we discover new scientific information. We need to hold our personal, *subjective* beliefs to this same *"open to new information"* standard when our *"subjective beliefs"* are confronted by new, conflicting information. We need to be open to the possibility of changing our *"subjective"* beliefs when we are presented with new information or ideas.

Changing our beliefs and opinions is very difficult for our childhood primitive ego because of its need to "always be right."

How Human Nature Complicates the Issue

In the *subjective* realm, human nature uses our ability to "think" about our "thinking" to create *subjective "oppositional" thinking.* The technical name is *dialectical thinking.*

Here is how it works ... it is human nature 101.

PRIMITIVE EGO PSYCHOLOGY

Our human brains are wired in such a way that *when person A comes up with a "subjective" thesis "A," person B will always come up with a "subjective" anti-thesis "B."*

As a result, the potential for the human mind to create *subjective oppositional thinking is* always present, and virtually unlimited.

When both person A and person B are;

- using dualistic thinking, and
- their childhood primitive egos are unconsciously using their subjective beliefs *to create their false - "self" identities*, and
- they both need to be "right" in order to protect those false "self"-identities,

it is easy to understand how they will almost certainly create conflict and violence in their relationships ... a violence that all-to-often moves out of their relationship into the larger world.

We can not present our subjective views, beliefs, opinions, assumptions, and values in the imperative voice of absolute truth.

We can not present our subjective views, beliefs, opinions, assumptions, and values in the imperative voice of absolute truth.

By the end of the century, there will be an estimated 11 billion people making hundreds of *subjective* statements a day to themselves and others. Multiply that number by 365 days a year, and you begin to see the potential for conflict and violence in the world is indeed almost infinite. I am convinced that the most important task facing humanity in the 21st Century is the creation of a non-dual human consciousness capable of transforming the conflict, extremism, and violence created by our dualistic childhood primitive ego and its need to always be "right" into a more compassionate and loving world.

Fortunately, the evolutionary growth needed in human consciousness can happen very quickly.

A Middlepath Consciousness

When both persons can bring an awakened, non-dual, middlepath consciousness to the conversation, they come to the conversation knowing they cannot *"win"* the argument. Why? Because there is no argument to be won. They understand that both ends of the polarity being discussed simply reflect the subjective values they each believe important ... not *absolute truths*!

The wisdom of an awakened consciousness always embraces that simple reality.

The goal of an awakened adult non-dual middlepath consciousness is creating a world of "mutual benefit" or "common good"..... a non-dual middlepath consciousness *knows* that all of our so-called "ideological beliefs are "subjective beliefs," not absolute truth.

Stated differently, an awakened adult non-dual consciousness understands that in the world of *"subjective" beliefs* there are no categories called right or wrong... it *knows* that all beliefs are *"subjective"* and that "no one wins until everyone wins."

How Does A Middlepath Consciousness Work In A Relationship

The best way to bring productive conversation into the subjective realm is through the use of *non-dual middlepath thinking*... i.e.,. a non-dual *middlepath consciousness*.

A *middlepath consciousness* is created when.......

- the persons on both sides of an issue are *open minded, non-dual thinkers* that intentionally look for the truths, and enduring values embedded in the other person's position.
- both persons find a way to *compromise and create a way forward* that best embraces the enduring values that exist in each person.
- both persons accept the reality that *their opinions and beliefs are subjective, not absolute truth.*
- both persons recognize the *middlepath reality that our human culture evolves best* when we can bring a *middlepath consciousness* to the conversation and intentionally search for compromise.

PRIMITIVE EGO PSYCHOLOGY

Life coaches and mental health counselors need to understand the concept and power of non-duality in the *subjective* world of human relationships. This is especially important when our client confronts us with their *"subjective"* beliefs in the *imperative voice of absolute truth*.

We'll take a closer look at why this is important in the next section.

WHY THESE CONCEPTS ARE IMPORTANT FOR LIFE COACHES AND MENTAL HEALTH COUNSELORS

Life coaching and mental health counseling are focused on two areas of growth;
1. *teaching* the client the skills and insights needed to achieve their goals and dreams, and
2. *helping* the client grow in self-awareness so the *unconscious* primitive ego beliefs, opinions, and worldviews they learned in childhood can become more fully conscious.

Awakening the client's consciousness will help them challenge their old ways of thinking about reality so they can more quickly achieve their dreams and life goals. Growth in self-awareness will help them tame their childhood primitive ego and embrace new beliefs and worldviews. Unfortunately, changing our beliefs and worldviews is a slow and difficult process. The client's ego used those childhood primitive ego beliefs and worldviews to construct his/her childhood survival skills, and their self-identity. Changing a childhood survival skill, a reality distorting belief from childhood, or a worldview requires a person to change their sense of *who they are; a very challenging task for the childhood primitive ego;* because the childhood primitive ego *does not like change.*

Changing who we *are* is often a slow and difficult process. It requires patience on the part of the client *and* the life coach or mental health counselor. It's easy for the life coach or mental health counselor to become impatient with the client's slow progress and begin to use "logic" to help the client get "unstuck". If they do, they sometimes unintentionally begin to push too hard for change. Change is a long and slow process. Pushing too hard for change in the client will only bring your life coaching or counseling relationship with the client to a premature end. The client will hear your words as criticism and search for a life coach/counselor that better "understands" them.

Effective life coaches and mental health counselors have learned to be patient. They know that beliefs, opinions, and worldviews change very slowly. While they always try to *encourage* change, they also acknowledge how difficult it can be for their clients to challenge old ways of thinking.

Here are some of the beliefs and worldviews life coaches commonly encounter in the childhood primitive ego thinking of their clients;

- *happiness* is found out there in the world
- this should not be happening to "*me*"!
- I *know* that already! You don't need to tell me… lack of vulnerability and humility
- You don't know the *childhood* or *family* I came from… I'm a victim of my childhood
- It's not my *fault*… blaming, powerless
- Life isn't *fair* … poor me, their sad "life story"
- Life is a *struggle*… nothing ever works out for me, another victim mentality
- The system *is rigged,* that's why it's not worth struggling, excuse for doing nothing, why bother, no hope,
- I need to be *liked* and *loved* by everyone…I need to be perfect, but I'm flawed therefore I'm unlovable whenever I try to be who I am,
- It's *not nice to say no*… I'm powerless to take care of myself and my own needs; I must care for others before myself. I've been conditioned from childhood to focus on the needs of others, not self.

- I'm not *smart enough, pretty enough, strong enough, I'm not "_____"*. I have very low self-esteem, I'm not lovable just as I am.
- I don't like it, but I can't help being a bit judgmental… *dualistic* black and white, either/or thinking
- It's me vs. the world… survival of the fittest… the *illusion of separateness*… the idea that "i" or "self" is separate from the rest of reality.
- Us vs. them, what's in it for "me" thinking created by the illusion of separateness.
- the need to be *"right"*
- *judgmental* worldviews of sexism, racism, homophobia… a sense of otherness or *"them"*

The self-limiting beliefs and opinions from the client's childhood are practically unlimited… *and most of them are unconscious*. The challenge of life coaching or counseling is helping the client *"see"* the lack of absolute truth in their beliefs and opinions… *without sounding critical, lecturing, opinionated, or judgmental.*

Dualistic thinking and the *illusion of separateness* worldviews are unconsciously embedded in the childhood conditioning of almost every client's childhood primitive ego. They are directly responsible for the creation of most of the inequality, greed, prejudice, judgment, destruction of human rights, pain and suffering, conflict, and violence

---

The self-limiting beliefs and opinions from the client's childhood are practically unlimited… and most of them are unconscious.

---

created in human history. They are worldviews that cannot be changed by logic alone. They cannot be changed by force. They will begin to change only when the client *has become more self-aware*. They will begin to change *when the client's values change*.

It's important for the life coach/counselor to remember... the worldviews, opinions, and beliefs from the client's childhood were used to create the survival skills needed by the client's childhood primitive ego to protect themselves, *and* create their self-identity. So be patient. Be prepared for the client to move slowly toward their goals and dreams. Changing one's self-identity can be a very slow and painful process. The client can feel "fragmented" and overwhelmed at times.

To summarize the above ideas;

- the challenge of a life coach /counselor is *patience* while continuing to actively offer the client support and encouragement as they struggle to become self-aware. This is especially important when the client appears to be "stuck" on the life coaching/counseling journey toward their dreams and life goals. The challenge is helping the client become aware of their unconscious childhood primitive ego's reality distorting, self-limiting... beliefs, opinions, and worldviews; to make them more conscious even when their childhood primitive ego would rather *"not" acknowledge them*!

- The goal of the life coach/counselor is to *"hold"* the client in a *safe, supportive, and encouraging environment* as the client struggles to awaken their consciousness and do the hard work of becoming more self-aware. It takes time to awaken our human consciousness. It's hard work. A work that can leave the person feeling *fragmented and confused* about who they are for a while; and often struggling with a deep *sense of loss*.

- Until the life coach or mental health counselor has done their own work to become self-aware; to understand their own childhood primitive ego, they will not understand how challenging it can be to evolve the beliefs, opinions, worldviews, and conditioning of childhood. They will not understand their client and the client's sense of "fragmentation", their uncertainty as to who they are, or the sense of loss their client might be feeling.

- The greatest gift the life coach /counselor can offer their clients... is their own growth in self-awareness... the ability to

- emotionally and cognitively walk in the client's shoes as they journey together toward the client's goals and dreams.
- There are no shortcuts on the path to self-awareness. Learning to see and tame the childhood primitive ego can be as difficult as Nasrudin's inability to see his donkey. Becoming self-aware is not a journey one can take alone. Like your client, the life coach or counselor's growth in self-awareness will require years of formal work including time with a well-trained life coach or mental health counselor, group counseling, and professional supervision.

WHERE TO BEGIN AS A LIFE COACH

Clients change their worldviews, beliefs, and values when the old ways of "seeing" the world no longer make sense to them; not when that change is forced upon them by others. Initially, creating common ground with the client is achieved by keeping the focus on their goals and dreams. Listening to what is important to the client, and avoiding the excessive use of logic.

- Logic uses a level of consciousness that too often only challenges the client's worldviews and beliefs. It's important to remind ourselves that the *primary objective of a client's childhood primitive ego* is to defend their worldviews and self-identity. Until they achieve some self-awareness, the client's childhood primitive ego will attempt to engage in conversations that end with *"them"* being *right*.

Don't go there. Ask questions. Listen carefully.

- *Fight "for"* the world your client dreams about creating and living, not *"against"* the worldview beliefs of their childhood primitive ego. Over time, as your client becomes more self-aware and begins to "see" the benefits and value of an awakened consciousness, it will be easier for them to "open" their worldviews and beliefs, and begin letting go of the unconscious self-limiting beliefs and conditioning of their childhood. In fact, it's not uncommon for a client to change their beliefs without the conscious awareness that their beliefs *have* changed.

The question I hear most often from life coaches and mental health counselors is *"how do I get my clients to grow in self-awareness? How do I help them "see" their unconscious primitive ego?"*

The answer I give them is this.

- Become more intentionally self-aware of *your own* primitive ego,
- Learn to pay attention to the energy *you* are sending into the world and the beliefs behind that energy,
- Pay attention to the emotional knee-jerk responses to the experiences *you have* as you experience life,
- Ask *yourself* "who do "*I*" want to become? What are *my* life goals? What kind of life do I dream about living?"
- As you grow in self-awareness as a life coach / counselor the meaning of "You can't teach what you don't know, and you can't lead a client any further into the wilderness of self-awareness than you've had the courage to go on your own journey" will become obvious and intuitive.

When *you* have struggled to grow in self-awareness, when *you* have done the work of awakening your adult consciousness, you will *know* how to help your clients become more self-aware. You'll know the answer to your question. The skills and insights learned from Primitive Ego Psychology in this Manifesto are designed to support *you, and your clients*, on that inward journey.

BECOMING AN EFFECTIVE LIFE COACH

If you long to live a life that *adds value to the lives of others, a life that matters,* you must be willing to intentionally embrace the deeper level of self-awareness necessary to tame the childhood beliefs and conditioning of your own childhood primitive ego.

The journey from primitive ego thinking to the awakened non-dual consciousness of a successful life coach/counselor is a life long journey. It is the most rewarding journey you will ever experience, but *you will never "arrive."* Awakening the human consciousness *will never be finished*. And most importantly, *it's a journey we can't take alone.*

Awakening our consciousness to the presence of our childhood primitive ego and growth in self-awareness is challenging and very difficult to achieve on our own. It requires the *mirroring or honest feedback* of a *supportive community*; a community that is dedicated and fully committed to the task of awakening *their* consciousness. Possibilities include personal therapy, professional supervision, group therapy, supportive friends, or family. Essentially, you will need a community that you trust will honestly mirror back to you *what they see...* as *you* do the work of becoming an awakened, self-aware, non-dual, awakened life coach/counselor.

But most importantly, it requires a deep, passionate desire to awaken our consciousness and tame our unconsciousness childhood primitive ego.

As I mentioned above, a primary way to become self-aware is a willingness to pay close attention to the energy you are sending into the world... and *the belief or assumptions behind that energy*. The willingness to ask your self the question "what's driving that energy." Where is it coming from? Where did I learn that? What experience taught me that belief?

And then, when you have paid attention to the energy you're sending into the world:

- Embrace the courage to fully own what you discover about yourselves;
- be totally honest with yourself when you discover those things that have been hidden inside your unconscious minds;
- those things you really don't like about yourself;
- those things you would rather ignore or deny about yourselves.

And trust me, *most of what you learn about yourself will be embarrassing and difficult to accept.* That's why your childhood primitive ego has hidden it in your unconscious.

As I have said throughout this Manifesto, intentional self-awareness is not a journey for the faint of heart. It's a long process, and it takes great courage. But the payoff is well worth the struggle of the journey. It a journey you will never regret having taken. It will provide the wisdom and insights you will need to help your client be successful on *their* journey toward *their* goals.

Practices For The Journey Toward Self-Awareness And Taming Your Childhood Primitive Ego

First, begin each day with a brief review of the key Primitive Ego Psychology Insights offered in this manifesto. These insights include:
- Subjective dualistic right/wrong "i" thinking is found only in the human mind.
- Categories of good/bad, or right/wrong *are not found in reality or nature.*
- Subjective *dualistic* categories of *"us vs. them"* are not found in the *unity and wholeness of nature.*
- Dualistic either/or thinking is a human illusion created in childhood by your childhood primitive ego and your client's childhood primitive ego.
- *Dualistic primitive ego "i" thinking* created by the illusions of separateness is the worldview that most creates judgmental thinking, prejudice, suffering, and conflict in your life and your client's life.
- Only awakened, non-dual *wholistic "we" thinking* will bring the compassion and unconditional love you and your client hunger to experience.
- Only *non-dual unity "we" thinking* will bring peace, happiness, success and meaning into your life and your client's life.
- Only *non-dual middlepath "we" thinking*; the ability to search for the truths and enduring values that exist on both sides of every issue, will ensure a successful future for you, your client and the relationships you have with others.
- Only a *non-dual unity consciousness* that openly embraces the diversity created by our universe will create the unconditional love, compassion, and meaning you and your client want to manifest in your lives.

Secondly, reaffirm the seven realities that you as a life coach and your clients, will need to embrace on the journey:
1. **We cannot *fix* the world, but** *together we can change the world*. We can grow and evolve. We *can* awaken our consciousness and become more self-aware.
2. **We are** *not alone in our desire to grow and awaken our consciousness*. We are part of a large and growing global community. The collective *human consciousness of our world is awakening.*
3. **The world needs the goals and dreams of all of us to create a better future.**
4. ***Life coaches and counselors* don't need to have all the answers.** *Our clients* don't need to have all the answers. We simply need to work every day to become more *non-dual, middlepath thinkers*. We need to *look for the truths on both sides* of every issue, to *pay attention to the energy* we are sending into the world when we find ourselves overly concerned with *being "right."* We need to recognize that the *illusion of separateness*, more than any other belief, will bring unhappiness and conflict into our lives.

5) **The change we need to manifest in the world will come from:**
   - those who are willing to *work toward their goals and dreams, and become more self-aware* so they can bring compassion and meaning into the world.
   - those who have the desire and *passion to live a more authentic life.*
   - those who are willing to work to *become more self-aware...more fully human.*
   - those who want their life to mean more than simply taking up space on this planet.
6. **We cannot change our clients, ourselves, or the world overnight, but change *will* begin the day;**
   - we have the courage and humility to look within and embrace deep self-awareness and acknowledge the beams in our own eyes,

- we begin to recognize the dark, dualistic, right/wrong, good/bad, judgmental energy we see in the world began inside our own hearts.
- we have the courage to take action to change the dualistic thinking created in our own minds.
- we challenge the illusion of separateness and begin the journey to intentionally create a compassionate "we" focused human culture that embraces the concept of "mutual benefit."

7. **Use middlepath thinking to support our growth in self-awareness.**
    - Until we intentionally increase our self-awareness and take the inner journey into the shadows of our inner-child psyche, our childhood primitive ego *will* continue to use unconscious dualistic thinking to create the violent categories of "us vs. them" in our world ... a violence that will continue to create unhappiness and conflict in the world ... and in our day to day lives.
    - Non-dual, middlepath thinking that searches for the truths found on both sides of every issue is a habit that can be learned and practiced every day. Over time, that habit will re-wire our brain and give birth to a true non-dual consciousness in us, and in our clients.

Until we intentionally increase our self-awareness and take the inner journey into the shadows of our inner-child psyche, our childhood primitive ego will continue to use unconscious dualistic thinking to create the violent categories of "us vs. them" in our world

---

8. **Remember the adage that says, "You can't reach those lands hidden just over the horizon by staring at the water."**
   - To bring the changes we would like to see in the world will require that we have the courage to *push off from the shore and journey together into the unknown.*
   - As a life coach or mental health counselor, that is the work that you are helping your clients embrace. It's not just helping them achieve their goals and dreams; it's helping them discover purpose and meaning in their lives… discovering the *meaningful life they came here to live.*

STAGES OF AWAKENING

The diagram below illustrates the work that we undertake as life coaches or mental health counselors. The *first three stages* we need to achieve to become more self-aware, evolve our human consciousness, become a successful life coach/counselor are;
- taming our primitive ego,
- intentional growth in self-awareness and
- embracing a middlepath consciousness.

Each stage in the diagram represents a sustainable *stage* of growth in consciousness, not a transitory *state* of consciousness. Each time we catch ourselves sliding back to an *earlier stage of consciousness* it is simply another opportunity to pay attention and become more self-aware. There is no failure, only learning, and growth. Life Coaching and mental health counseling is about moving inward and deeper……*always.*

Stages 1-3 reflect the work we are embracing as life coaches and mental health counselors when we answer the call to add value to the lives of our client's and the world. A life coach/counselor is about adding value to the life of a client so that client can go into the world as a ripple on the pond of your teaching…….and begin adding value to the world and the lives of others as they work to achieve their dreams and goals.

This is the work we are called to embrace as life coaches. This is the task you have committed your life to achieving. The goal? Improving the quality of our client's life. Creating healthy relationships for a more compassionate world. Creating a more evolved, mature, awakened, universal humanity.

What kind of energy are you sending into the world? What's the belief or assumption driving that energy?

It's that simple... and that challenging.

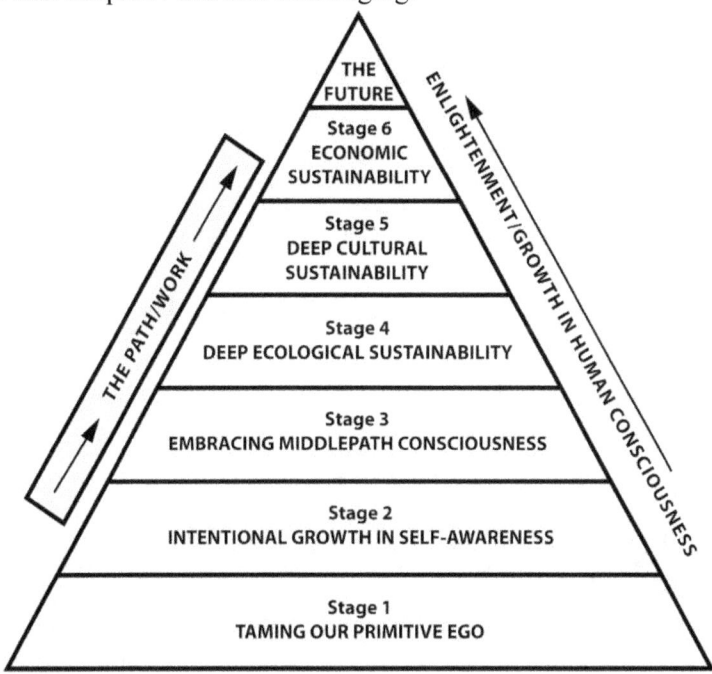

STAGE 1: TAMING THE PRIMITIVE EGO

- Learn to let go of the childhood primitive ego's need *for black-and-white thinking*... the need to be *"right"* and the *illusion of separateness*. We grow in self-awareness when we learn to embrace a more gray, *non-dual human* consciousness ... a more wholistic, non-tribal us vs. them, non-dualistic way of thinking ... in other words, the *non-duality of the universe* taught by modern scientists and all of humanity's great spiritual teachers, saints, and sages.

- Recognize that humanity is an interdependent, interconnected, non-dual oneness or unity called *"we"* and *"us"*... not a tribal,

fragmented dualistic worldview collection of categories called "*us vs. them*". Reality is unity and oneness.
- Increase our ability to recognize that our separate "i" is one of humanity's more dangerous illusions. Recognize that we can best achieve growth in self-awareness and the awakening of our human consciousness by the rational ability to empty our primitive ego of its illusion that our *"self"* is an object separate from the rest of reality. It's not! The *illusion of separateness* is the taproot that feeds greed and violence in the world.
- •Let go of our childhood primitive ego's reality distorting beliefs, and its never-ending need to be "right."

STAGE 2: INTENTIONAL GROWTH IN SELF-AWARENESS

Pay attention to the energy you are sending into the world. Always ask yourself the question "where is that energy coming from? What belief or opinion is driving that energy?

STAGE 3: EMBRACING A MIDDLEPATH CONSCIOUSNESS

Stage three reflects a stage of consciousness in which one has achieved the ability to embrace an authentic *middlepath consciousness*. The *emptiness of ego* needed to;
- abandon one's *need to be right*, and
- intentionally search with an open mind for the truths contained on both sides of every issue… because no one is smart enough to be wrong, or right, all of the time.

WHY I WROTE THIS MANIFESTO

I wrote this Manifesto as a way of saying thank you for the wisdom and insights I've learned from my many teachers and especially from my clients over the years. Both have taught me most of what I know about the art of life coaching and mental health counseling.

The insights and skills of Primitive Ego Psychology contained in this Manifesto were born in the crucibles of growth and change... a lifetime of experience and a thirty-year journey helping clients awaken their consciousness and accomplish the difficult work of taming their childhood primitive ego through growth in self-awareness.

Thank you for taking the time to read this manifesto. I sincerely hope it has been helpful.

I encourage your feedback and comments.

Dick Rauscher
Redmond, Oregon 2016 Redmond, Oregon 2016

ADDENDUM: WHY I BELIEVE PRIMITIVE EGO PSYCHOLOGY IS SO IMPORTANT

The world is on a path that many believe is taking us toward a future that we really don't want to experience... for ourselves, or our children and grandchildren. Life coaching and mental health counseling offer powerful tools and skills to support the awakening of our human consciousness; powerful insights for growth in self-awareness.

- We know we are on a path that is *not sustainable.*
- We know that the illusion of *separateness is creating the greed* that fuels our broken global economic system.
- We know that we *are running out of time* to embrace the changes that will be needed if we are to create a sustainable future.
- We know our dependence on petroleum and natural gas needs to end "*now.*"
- We know that the multinational corporations, Wall Street, the petroleum energy corporations, and the 1% are *not going to give up their access to wealth and power voluntarily*. We know they will fight to the bitter end even though they have known for years that our greed based economic system has us on a collision course with a future that will create immense dislocation, starvation, and suffering.
- We know that unless we work together to force the changes and the sustainable deconstruction of our current economic systems, nothing is going to change in time to avoid the greatest threat to

human civilization and human survival in the last 65 million years....global warming and global climate change.
- We know the path to a *sustainable future will require the awakening and transformation of human consciousness discussed in this manifesto.* There is no other path for humanity that will confront the built-in pathologies and destructive power of our current greed based economic systems.

As professional Life Coaches and Mental Health Counselors, you have the ability and opportunity to support the awakening and transformation of our human consciousness by confronting the dualism created inside our collective childhood primitive ego's dualistic thinking and the illusion of separateness. You have the ability and opportunity to help others awaken their consciousness and grow in self-awareness... to help your clients tame the narcissism and self-focus of their childhood primitive ego.

Until that happens, we will continue to support the greed and self-interest of our current economic systems. Our separate "i" consciousness will continue to win out over the collective, interconnected, interdependent "we" consciousness our world needs to embrace.

- Until we have transformed our separate *"i" consciousness* to a collective *"we" consciousness,* the concept of *"mutual benefit"* and *"common good"* will lack the energy and passion needed to embrace the changes in lifestyle that all of us will need to make.
- *"Mutual benefit"* and *"common good"* are simply ways of saying that hunger has been eliminated from our planet. They are ways of saying that we are ready to voluntarily begin sharing the wealth and resources that we enjoy with the rest of humanity. *"Mutual benefit"* and *"common good"* have the power to transform human culture, and our current global economic system, into deeply sustainable systems.
- Only when our human culture and our global economic systems fully embrace *"mutual benefit" and deep sustainability,* will we have the wisdom, compassion, insights, or empathy to include the other living beings and living systems that share the planet with us. Only then will we be capable of living in right

relationship with nature. Only then will we have the deep sustainability needed to save our planet and it's diverse life forms from the sixth extinction.

- Deep sustainability is necessary in our human *economic system*. Deep sustainability is urgently needed in our shared *ecological systems*. Taming the childhood primitive ego and growth in self-awareness are essential if our goals and dreams include the creation of a sustainable future. That sustainable future can happen only if;
- you and I have awakened our consciousness,
- you and I have embraced *non-dual thinking*,
- you and I have recognized the *illusion of separateness* as a profoundly dangerous distortion of reality, and finally, when
- you and I have embraced the reality that *we are all interconnected and interdependent* on one another; on all of the other living beings, and all of the living ecosystems that make up our planetary life support system.

Summary

I believe the ideas and concepts presented in this manifesto, are not just good ideas. I am convinced they are *absolutely essential* for the survival of our human civilization and our human culture. Our environmental scientists are warning that they may even be essential for the very survival of our human species.

If we are to survive the challenges facing us as a species, *everything will need to change*. But the most important change will be the transformation of our own human consciousness. *If we don't learn to tame our childhood primitive ego and its never-ending focus on "me" and "my," the future for our struggling planetary support system and our species will be grim.*

We live on a finite and fragile planet. It will not survive the greed of our global economic system and the dangerous illusion of "*unlimited economic expansion*." We need to stand together and become the change our children and grandchildren need us to become if they are to survive.

A *just* and *compassionate* world will require all of us to get involved.

As professional *life coaches, students of life coaching*, and *mental health counselors* you, more than any others, have the skills, training, and commitment to awaken the consciousness of your clients, add value the lives of others, and in the process create a more awakened and compassionate world.

I believe Primitive Ego Psychology is a powerful professional resource that will help us achieve that goal.

ABOUT THE AUTHOR

Dick Rauscher is an experienced author, professional life coach, certified AAPC Fellow, and NYS licensed mental health counselor. He is the writer/editor of the Stonyhill-Nugget Newsletter/Blog offering practical examples in the use of primitive ego theory for the intentional evolution and awakening of the human consciousness, and to improve the quality of everyday life.

Dick has a lifetime of training and experience helping people achieve their life goals, success, happiness, creating healthy relationships and creating deeper meaning in their lives. In addition to his writing, Dick offers one-on-one personal life coaching and seminars.

www.ingramcontent.com/pod-product-compliance
Lightning Source LLC
Chambersburg PA
CBHW061221180526
45170CB00003B/1100